THE PERSON BEHIND THE BRAND

LONNIE JOHNSON

Written by Annette Whipple

Illustrated by Gary Boller

TABLE OF CONTENTS

A Starfish Book

SEAHORSE PUBLISHING

Teaching Tips for Caregivers:

As a caregiver, you can help your child succeed in school by giving them a strong foundation in language and literacy skills and a desire to learn to read.

This book helps children grow by letting them practice reading skills.

Reading for pleasure and interest will help your child develop reading skills and will give your child the opportunity to practice these skills in meaningful ways.

- Encourage your child to read on their own at home.
- Encourage your child to practice reading aloud.
- Encourage activities that require reading.
- Establish a reading time.
- Talk with your child.
- Give your child writing materials.

Teaching Tips for Teachers:

Research shows that one of the best ways for students to learn a new topic is to read about it.

Before Reading

- Read the "Words to Know" and discuss the meaning of each word.
- Read the back cover to see what the book is about.

During Reading

- When a student gets to a word that is unknown, ask them to look at the rest of the sentence to find clues to help with the meaning of the unknown word.
- Ask the student to write down any pages of the book that were confusing to them.

After Reading

- Discuss the main idea of the book.
- Ask students to give one detail that they learned from the book by showing a text-dependent answer from the book.

LONNIE JOHNSON —SUPER SOAKER

Young Lonnie Johnson liked to **tinker**.

He liked to see how things worked.

Lonnie and his friends made a go-kart from scraps.

It was not perfect, but it was fun.

Lonnie kept tinkering. He built a robot for a contest.

Moving air lifted the robot's arms and legs.

Lonnie won first place.

Lonnie went to college.

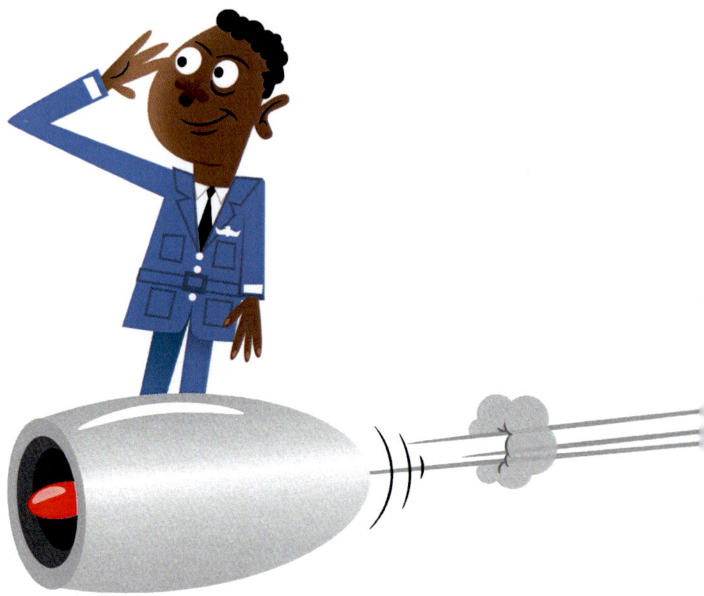

He served in the Air Force.

Lonnie got a job at NASA.

He still tinkered at home.

One night, Lonnie was working in his bathroom.

He tried to fix a pump.

Water shot out.

Lonnie got an idea for making a powerful squirt gun.

Lonnie tinkered and tinkered.

He built a working **model**.

Lonnie gave the **prototype** to his daughter.

It soaked her friends.

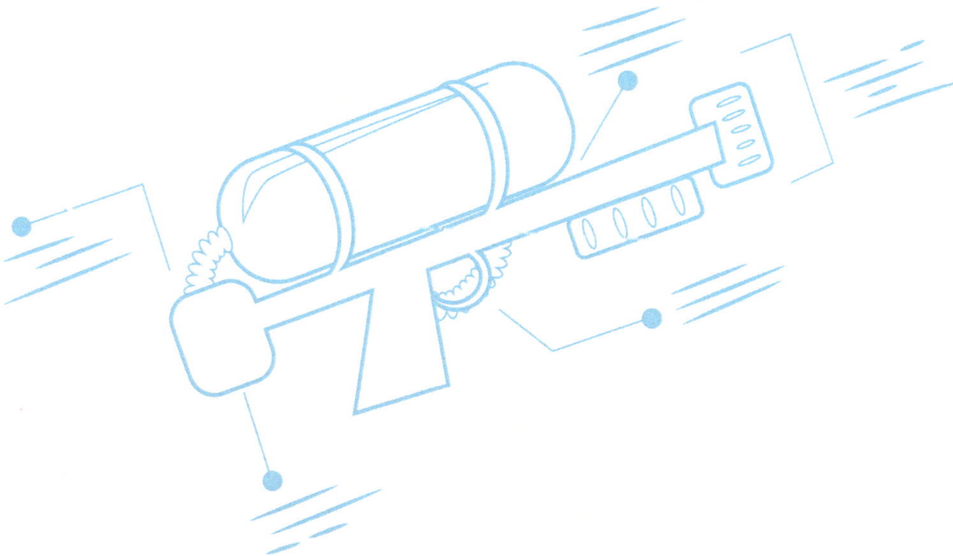

Lonnie wanted to build water blasters to sell.

Some people said his ideas would not work.

Lonnie made lots of models.

It took a long time.

After seven years, Lonnie built a better model.

He showed it to a **company**.

The company wanted to **produce** the toy.

Lonnie's model became the Super Soaker water blaster.

It uses air to spray water as far as 50 feet (15 meters).

Kids love it!

People still play with Super Soakers around the world.

Lonnie Johnson is a successful **inventor**.

He is successful because he kept tinkering.

LONNIE JOHNSON

in 2016

He is successful because he did not give up.

Words to Know

company (KUHM-puh-nee): an organization that makes and sells products or services

inventor (in-VEN-tuhr): a person who creates something new

model (MAH-duhl): something built as an example; a thing built to show how something will work

produce (pruh-DOOS): to make something, often in a factory and often for sale

prototype (PROH-tuh-tipe): the first version of an invention

tinker (TING-kur): to make small changes to something to fix or improve it, to experiment with it, or to see how it works

Index

Comprehension Questions

1. Lonnie Johnson used __________ to move the arms and legs of his robot.
a. water
b. air
c. strings

2. Lonnie tried to fix a __________ in his bathroom.
a. water blaster
b. light
c. pump

3. Lonnie gave the first water blaster to his __________.
a. neighbors
b. daughter
c. brother

4. True or false: Lonnie built a bicycle with his friends.

5. True or false: Lonnie worked on the Super Soaker for seven years.

Answers:
1. b, 2. c, 3. b, 4. False, 5. True

About the Author

Annette Whipple celebrates curiosity through her books. She wrote *The Laura Ingalls Wilder Companion*, *Whooo Knew? The Truth About Owls*, and *Quirky Critter Devotions*. She lives with her family in Pennsylvania where she appreciates the natural beauty around her. Get to know Annette at www.AnnetteWhipple.com.

About the Illustrator

Gary Boller lives in the glorious countryside in Hampshire, UK, with his wife and two children, one Chihuahua, and four cats. He always doodled as a kid, even on his parents' walls, and loved the comics of the day. Gary also loves music and has played double bass in bands. He has toured all over Europe many times and the USA twice. He's currently learning fiddle, much to the annoyance of his pets.

Written by: Annette Whipple
Illustrated by: Gary Boller
Designed by: Under the Oaks
Editor: Kim Thompson
Production manager:
Candice Campbell

Library of Congress PCN Data
Lonnie Johnson / Annette Whipple
The Person Behind the Brand
ISBN 979-8-8945-9117-9 (hard cover)
ISBN 979-8-8945-9122-3 (paperback)
ISBN 979-8-8945-9132-2 (EPUB)
ISBN 979-8-8945-9127-8 (eBook)
Library of Congress Control Number: 2024946244

Printed in the U.S.A./CP112025

Seahorse Publishing Company
www.seahorsepub.com

Published in the United States
Seahorse Publishing
PO Box 771325
Coral Springs, FL 33077

SEAHORSE PUBLISHING